Words from My Mind

The poetry of Daniel Dennehy

Stream~lines

an imprint of

Riverhaven

www.RiverhavenBooks.com

Published in the United States
by Riverhaven,
www.RiverhavenBooks.com

ISBN: 978-1-951854-02-7

Printed in the United States of America
by Country Press, Lakeville, Massachusetts

First Edition, 2019

Artwork by Daniel Dennehy
Edited and designed by Stephanie Lynn Blackman
Whitman, Massachusetts

Stream~Lines, an imprint of Riverhaven
781-447-0167
www.RiverhavenBooks.com
18 Pearl Street, Whitman, MA 02382

Dedication:

I dedicate this book to everyone, everywhere,
no matter who you are.
And, most importantly,
to my amazing nephew Luke,
and to the people who always told me I could.

"Hope is the thing with feathers
that perches in the soul and sings the tune without the
words and never stops at all."
~Emily Dickinson

"Let me be as a feather.
Strong with purpose,
Yet light at heart
Able to bend.

And, tho I might
Become frayed,
Able to pull myself
Together again."
~Anita Sams

Table of Contents

The Forest

The forest trees glimmer under the sun,
deer rest under the bushes,
and the rabbits run away from coyotes in fear.
The forest is peaceful,
no lawn mowers, no generators,
or yelling kids, or revving engines.
No people, no disturbance.
It is just the wind and I, the trees and I,
and the blue evening sky.
Some creatures are older than I, and some much older.
Little teacup-sized critters, and some the size of boulders.
The forest lies in peace, away from the public,
a hermit of itself, its only friend is the animals
and the wind blowing south.
The forest glimmers like a stage in an opera house,
and the winds screams like the high notes of a violin.
The forest is a house of wonders, secrets, and peace.
A temple in nature, just without a priest.
The birds fly around doves on Heaven's stairs,
and the deer wake up and eat without a care.
The bugs light up in the shade, and the
vegetation around turns a bright jade.
The tree gives us life
and never expects a thank you,
and depends on itself to survive.
This forest is peace, and humanity would cease
if this wasn't in our big blue home,
but we should let these animals live in peace
and leave them alone. Enjoy the nature and its beauty,
without killing these innocent creatures so cruelly

The Bright Tree

There was a tree that never had to fight
     for sun and sky,
      brisk air and light.
But as it stood out taller than others,
     it got its fair share of rain.
As the bright tree stood, it shrugged off pain,
     stayed strong,
      learned from its mistakes.

When the next rain fell, he put on a hood.

This tree was clever and kind,
     admired by all,
      however, the rain kept falling.
The tree decided life's not about waiting f
     or the storm to pass.
So the tree bowed to its dance partner, the wind,
     and soon after the birds and bugs
      started dancing inside its core.

Not long after, the deer caught along,
     and spun and sang
      their own unique songs.
And when a full moon lit up the sky,
     the wolves added to the forest melody.
Racoons emerged from their homes,
     and played until
      the moon went down.

As the night set to sleep, a new sound was heard.

The animals all feared the noise and
     when big and mighty shadows scurried
      across the woods, the animals hid (as well they should).
And the shadows emerged
     with gleaming unique skin.

But the Bright Tree stayed in place,
        protected its home,
        guarded it's base.

As the tree stood, it watched.

These invaders started to gather,
        with happy and cheerful grins.
        And minutes after a crowd followed along.
The tree became a hopeful place where people danced
        and sang funny songs.
The Bright Tree continued to grow.
        As years have passed,
        people of young and old still come to dance and sing.

As time passed, respect grew.

And the branches on the tree grew to embrace
        people of all races, cultures,
        religions, and genders.
They remembered to smile and cherish the ones they loved.
        When the forest was quiet, the animals still gathered.
All of nature understood the
        lesson of the Bright Tree –

                Dance in the rain,
                  be flexible,
      be strong – even when the wind blows fiercely,
          and be a place of shelter for all.

The Lighthouse

A lighthouse lies alone and cold on the ocean shore, stays away from the others, and sat there bored.
Ships avoid it and steer away on the west.
The lighthouse becomes ugly and abandoned – it doesn't care anymore.
The lighthouse is living its life, like it's a chore.
The lighthouse carries on, staying away from the others, but still gives a smile to his brothers.
The ocean laughs at the lighthouse – how lonely can someone be?
And the beach scoffs behind the ocean, pretending to think the same thing.
But the lighthouse is brave.
It stands confidently in front of the raging waves. It is a leader that helps pave the way for the land.
It helps the ships get by and is a wall
to the old flimsy and frail village that lies behind it. The lighthouse keeps hope, continues giving,
and helps the less fortunate cope.
The lighthouse is a leader and creates it own trail.
And even though the lighthouse is left out, and demeaned, it refuses to be mean.
It keeps a cool head and becomes wiser.
It only speaks the truth, but it says that in itself is a lie. The lighthouse waits on the side,
and even though he is treated so bad, he still survives.

Waves

There are some waves,
flowing softly in the morning sun.
I see some kids running by, having fun.
The dune grass flows silently,
and the winds flow gently on my face.
The trees across the street dance with pride,
and the baby birds fly away after saying goodbye.
These waves are a home to millions of majestic things,
and a majority of them we have never seen.
But these waves aren't clean.
Careless sailors toss their beer cans,
or kids put their candy wrappers under the sand.
These waves are not clean, and I'm sad to say
that a lot of these majestic creatures will never be seen again.
The seals pop their heads out of the water,
and plastic bag pieces are stuck on their face.
Fish jump out of the water, plastic stuck to their gills.
Slowly the beach becomes less of a thrill.
But I see some men with their hands scooping the ground,
picking up straws and wrappers pound by pound.
The sun shines brightly and sets when they leave,
but the hearts on these folks,
help these majestic creatures breathe.

Courage

Courage to stand out.
Courage to chase your dreams.
Courage to not listen to what people want you to be.

Courage to laugh,
the feeling of being free,
courage to not only see what I want to see.

Courage to thank, courage to trust,
having that courage is always a plus.

Courage to fail,
the will to succeed,
the courage to be who we want to be.

The courage to do despite what others say,
the courage to take anyone as your brother and grant them fair play.
The courage to help, the courage to accept.
We have courage.
This is known to be;
The toughest courage there could be.

The Gleaming (Polish Invasion of World War Two)

In an old, crumbling town,
everyone's been feeling down.
Children crying in despair,
planes bombing from the air.
Shops are plundered,
homes are leveled,
cadavers in the street,
I counted several.
When will this stop?

No one knows.

Blood rivers continue to flow.
The flowers in the ground refuse to grow.
The smoky sky refuses to glow.
I want food, but I don't want to eat.
I am so tired yet cannot sleep.
The pain continues.
When does it stop?

No one knows.

The cadavers are beginning to rot.
I'm in so much pain, I cannot feel.
The skin on my body is beginning to peel.
This is a war, not a simple feud.
A deep hatred, far from new.
The gravel on the road is broken like our hearts.
So much pain,
when does it stop?

No one knows.

A father carries a little boy, a toy in his hand, onto a bus.
He doesn't understand; he never fussed.
But his mother weeps; her hands in her face,

dry tears, crackling lungs from the smoke in the air.
They haven't showered in weeks.
No one is here to help us.
Does anyone still care?

No one knows.

We have to flee, before our bodies run limp,
from starvation that has plagued our nation since...
Dusk has arrived, a new fight for our lives
has come, we have no time to cry.
The air is still thick with smog, and filled
with a stomach-churning odor.
The weather is warm, yet it still feels polar.
It is the dead of dusk; the pasture is still.
Will anyone help?

No one knows.

Our hearts are pounding, yet we proceed up the hill.
No tanks in sight, our feet are silent as the night.
Stay calm; refuse to go in fright.
The sun is rising, the color of blood;
if you make one wrong move; you may be done.
Stride in courage, stride in God's will.
If the Angel of Death is near, stand completely still.
Is the end near? Can we make it out?

No one knows.

Stay calm, do not pout.
The light is near, do not fear.
There are no enemies here.
Your bones may hurt, your stomach may ache,
but come into the light, you will be safe.
We have to continue, one last haul,
down the hill, do not fall.
Will is soon end?

No one knows.

Enemies on the east, and tanks on the west.
Keep looking forward until we can rest.
Travel in the shadows, tanks are near,
zip your mouth, we are all in fear.
I know you're hungry, there is no cure.
One more push, keep it up. You can endure
You can hear the tires turning, the metal grinding,
that big red crest on the side brightly shining.
Is that a town ahead with proud buildings and glowing signs,
vendors of delectable food, so divine?

No one knows.

A faithful rush forward,
do not fall behind.
But my legs are falling,
my heart is slowing,
my breath is hardly flowing.
My mind is fading,
and my body has no
energy left for me.
But I see a light and with no spite
I continue to walk ahead,
I feel so safe and ready to brace
for whatever is ahead.
But I have a feeling that this gleaming
is all just in my head.
Is it?

No one knows.

A Champion's Cudgel

A victor shines above,
gives his community all of his love,
and protects their lives with his.
He used to be a lonely soul,
walking down a lonely road
with sorrow written on his face.
But he had found a place
which gave him amity and embrace.
He prayed and sang,
with pride and grace,
and God shined his light on him.
So he walked to the house for the old,
in the freezing cold,
to find a heart of gold.
And as he went back home,
he put on a face of pride and bold,
and gave the last of his food away.
He was hungry the next day,
but when he went to pray
he had found out something new today.
His peers gave him a smile of love,
and as he looked above,
a dove shined in the roof of the chapel.
And a figure rose who had known
of the deeds that he had done.
And as he went home,
he came to know that the fridge he had
was full.
And with grace, he ran to the bank,
to find that he was rich.
But with his new wealth, happiness,
and health he prayed even more.
He was a charitable soul,
and was so mellow,
he would never scold.
And as he grew old,

he stayed happy and bold,
and gave most of his money away.
And so it is told, when he grew cold,
his body rose above.
A shining light,
dove fluttering and swerving with might,
he laid at rest with God.
And so a cudgel flew down,
and the wind moved around,
and the cudgel was made from
the love of his soul.
Later that day, the town gathered and prayed,
celebrating the life of the champion.
And all their souls were filled with love,
and turned mighty and bold.
And his cudgel paved the way.
We are all a work of God,
His eyes always would see,
someone who wasn't perfect,
but in heaven they could be.
The love they gave to others,
and their constant yet infectious care.
Their dreams in life,
and their will to get them there.
We are all a work of God,
an abstract one indeed,
but just remember to give
love and charity to others,
and never develop greed.

It's Your Life

You live the way everyone else wants you to live,
people's opinions stab you in the gut like a shiv.
You are a snowflake on the hot summer pavement,
melting rapidly in the sun's gaze.
But you have God's praise, blessed with potential to be an eagle,
that flies among the hares.
You may embrace God's love and bright shining care.
The world is yours, but from now on learning shall not be a chore.
And absorbing the endless intelligence may not be a bore.
You're young; the life shines in your eyes, be unique,
and do it with pride.
While not everyone will accept you,
their opinion is their right.
Keep that chin up, stride with pride.
Love the trees, tip your hat as you pass by the bees,
and let that single tear of joy fall
as you silently admire the sea.

Ten years later...
In the car we passed by the meadow; I saw your eye glitter.
When you were a kid you were so insecure,
Even though I know you're scared
that huge ring will definitely fit her.
I can't believe you grew up on me like that.
You were once a little sapling, and now you're beginning to sprout...
You're so special to me, like fish to the sea,
or honey to the bees.
But you need to fly away, gather your guts and say,
"Will you marry me?"
It is so hard to spit out, but when you remember
that your tree is ready to sprout, it will finally come out.

The day of the wedding...
What a beautiful bride!
She is the one, I can tell by her eyes.
Now, you made your mother cry. And me too.

But happy tears – they feel like holy water.
Your father in-law is so happy, he can't believe
that girl is his daughter.
But I just wanted to say again, that I love you.
You used to hide in your room, an insecure little goblin.
But now you are a fierce lion, getting ready to roar,
and now you are preparing for another big score.

Fifty years later...
Son, I'm ready to leave now.
But before I do,
I need to say
I am so proud of you.
You have a life ahead of you now; I have nothing left to be.
I was a chapter in the book of life,
but now you're the next ones to read.

Don't Wait Up for Me

Don't wait up for me, but don't jump ahead.
I will be scared if on my own.
I'm only a baby compared to you.
Care for me; I need more time to grow.
Continue the songs you wrote,
but keep me at your side.
I am too young to say goodbye.

Keep me in your arms from here on out.
Give me your love, and I'll have no doubts.
I want to be like you some day,
but all I can do is prepare, watch, and pray.
Show me around the world's open house,
but wait for me, I still skip like a mouse.
I'm a little faster now, but I still need you.
Keep that roof over my head.
And can you please make me dinner and make my bed?
I'm still young, but shot of a cannon I am,
I can be powerful if I can just grab your hand.

Growing older now, I have some wisdom,
but I still need your love.
And if I cannot make it on my own
Quite yet, know that I'm not fully grown.
I miss home. Can I come over soon?
Oh, and make sure when I lift off the ground,
you follow me to the moon.

I'm grown now, and my wings have formed.
My soul produces more energy than the Earth's core.
I'm a spaceship, ready to take off.
I can complete my dreams, and I've weighed the costs.
This is my final form, my peak,
Though there's still more knowledge I must seek.
I landed aboard this lonely road
to find new paths and knowledge to know.

You may think it's over, but I'm not yet my best.
Watch me grow from just a tree into a forest.
This is my voice, watch me do good deeds,
The key to my potential, steer away from greed.

I'm a forest, for however long I'll stand.
It is my time to teach, to hold another's hand
and show them my songs, and make their bed.
I won't wait up, but I won't jump ahead.
Like a bird teaching it's young how to soar,
I'll be there to guide them so they can grow more.
This is my voice, I will use it for good,
in God's holy name, as you've taught me I should.

Across the Stars

A rocket ship will take you far
to see a crater,
quasar,
star,

constellations, ultra bright,
any planet,
comet,
meteorite.

It is time to fly,
our rocket ship away,
flying, soaring
today is the day.

The Moon

The moon has no light of its own.
It's cold and dark
and dead as stone.
But absorbing light
from the bursting sun,
it shows its purpose when the day is done.

Never forget: You may not know your purpose yet.
But that doesn't mean that you don't have one.

Landed!

Neil, with his space gear prepared,
landed on the moon's surface.

Wingless
weightless
floating like dust,

Stars
atoms,
and matter among us

Drifting silently,
we wait to walk the unknown roads ahead.

The Galaxy Above

The planets in their galaxy,
brightly dotted stars I see.
In a pattern one by one,
revolving quickly 'round the sun.
Gravity keeps me set in place,
as I silently spin in the grasp of space.

The planets around us we should all know,
'round and 'round in space they go.
Mercury, Venus, Jupiter, and Mars –
None of these planets are too far.
These spheres silently float we know,
as 'round and 'round the sun they go.

The Truth

Our society needs the truth,
sweet or not.
Because when vulnerable children buy into it,
we begin to rot.

Even though it may not seem to be,
truth is helpful,
valuable, and positive.
Leading us towards the right path.
Because once we gain truth,
we will never go back.

Our Influence

We may not realize how a kind word spoken
May lift some heart that is sad and broken
The truth indeed may open the eyes
of a person distant from facts or blinded by lies.
Anyone can reach for the hands of one
who cannot feel the struggle of others,
or touch the hearts of the ones
who cannot feel the vibrations
and the beautiful moments of life.
Anyone can caution those
who use words as knives
or cause others to struggle.
Anyone can spread hope and joy
into other's lives, and reflect
light rather than darkness.

This Isn't Goodbye

Even though this book is over
I will come back again.
The sun will shine,
the constellations glare,
the tides shall rise and fall,
and Earth will spin and rotate around the sun.
May the fun stay as the party of life has just begun.
The breeze will flow, the trees will sway,
the music on the radio will still play.
Yes, this book is over, but my words have just begun.
The first steps of my career are still far from done.
So, thank you, all.
You've been so great.
Keep on shining, vict'ry awaits.

www.ingramcontent.com/pod-product-compliance
Lightning Source LLC
Chambersburg PA
CBHW020957030426
42339CB00005B/137